Experiencing God's Overwhelming Peace During Hard Times

KNOW GOD – EXPERIENCE PEACE

PEARL NSIAH-KUMI

Gotham Books

30 N Gould St.
Ste. 20820, Sheridan, WY 82801
https://gothambooksinc.com/

Phone: 1 (307) 464-7800

© 2024 *Pearl Nsiah-Kumi*. All rights reserved.

No part of this book may be reproduced, stored in a retrieval system, or transmitted by any means without the written permission of the author.

Published by Gotham Books (October 22, 2024)

ISBN: 979-8-3304-4157-0 (P)
ISBN: 979-8-3304-4158-7 (E)

Because of the dynamic nature of the Internet, any web addresses or links contained in this book may have changed since publication and may no longer be valid.

The views expressed in this work are solely those of the author and do not necessarily reflect the views of the publisher, and the publisher hereby disclaims any responsibility for them.

Dedication

This book is dedicated to my children, church family, medical team, and friends around the world, who have prayed me through this experience. Their love, support, dedication, and prayers have made this book possible. May God's blessings be upon you and yours.

Pearl Nsiah-Kumi

Acknowledgements

Many thanks to God for making this story possible by allowing the experience. Thank you, God! Thanks to my editor, Joanne Sher, for editing my writings and for her encouragement. Thank you, Joanne.

Finally, to praying friends and family, thank you for your ongoing support and prayers. Please don't stop; keep them coming.

TABLE OF CONTENTS

Dedication i
Acknowledgements ii

EXPERIENCING GOD'S OVERWHELMING PEACE

How It All Started 1
It's My Birthday 2022 2
What A Difference A Year Can Make 4
Praying Pastors: 5
In Remission, Whoot, Whoot! 6
My Chemo Side Effects 7
The Abundant Life 9
What A Difference A Year Makes; It's My Birthday Again - 2023 11
God's Provision 13
Last Day Of Treatment – December 7, 2023 14

IS IT OR IS IT NOT OVER?

I'm Home Now 18
Christmas 2023 With Family 20
More pictures for your enjoyment! 21
Six Months After Treatment 37

iii

EXPERIENCING GOD'S OVERWHELMING PEACE

How It All Started

Eight years ago, in 2016, I was diagnosed with lymphoma that originated from the left breast. For the treatment, I elected to undergo radiation instead of chemotherapy. And for that, I had five radiation sessions per week for three weeks, a total of fifteen sessions. That was supposed to have been enough. I was followed up twice a year, alternating between the radiology oncologist and the medical oncologist. My follow-up exams were usually palpation for enlarged lymph nodes. PET scans were not recommended since they could expose me to more radiation, but the palpations never showed any new enlarged lymph nodes.

It's My Birthday 2022

In 2022, for my birthday, family and friends took me out for lunch. It was fun and I was in good health. It never crossed my mind that 2023 could be, and was going to be different. Below is the 2022 celebration:

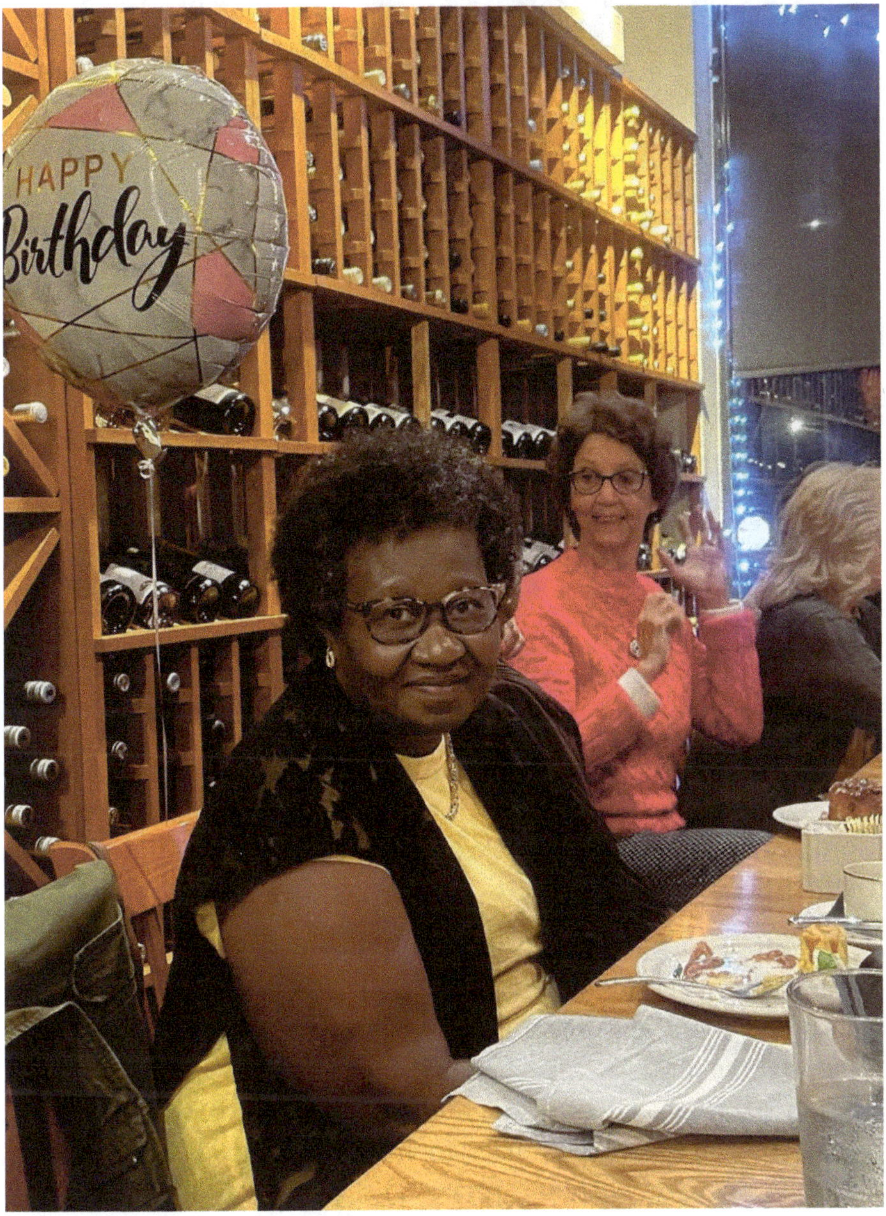
HAPPY
Birthday

What A Difference A Year Can Make

Come July 2023, nine months after the 2022 celebration, I reported to the emergency room with severe abdominal pain that warranted an abdominal scan.

The scan showed pancreatitis, an abdominal mass, and another mass behind the heart. This warranted a visit to the oncologist; he ordered further scans of my chest and abdomen, to be followed by a PET Scan at a later date.

The chest scan showed enlarged nodes behind the lungs, warranting a chest scan with contrast. That report led to a consult with the thoracic surgeon with the possibility of obtaining a biopsy; the biopsy was obtained under general anesthesia on 07/26/2023, and I was diagnosed with Diffuse large B-cell lymphoma of intra-abdominal lymph nodes. But in all of this, God gave me an overwhelming peace. That peace made me wonder whether I was all right, and wondered why I wasn't crying.

Actually, during one visit, my oncologist was surprised at my attitude; he said to me, "You don't seem worried." I responded: "No." It was because I knew many people were praying for me, and God had reminded me of other times when He had provided for me and put family and friends around me for encouragement. Oh, how I wish everyone knew my amazing God.

On August 02, 2023, I had a PET Scan that showed this lymphoma to be more aggressive than what I had in 2016. Treatment options were discussed; after my oncologist had consulted with his team, they decided that chemotherapy was the way to go. I was prescribed a regimen consisting of six different medications: ... Rituximab, Cyclophosphamide, Hydroxydaunomycin, Oncovin, Prednisone (RCHOP) for a total of six doses to be administered intravenously every three weeks. A subcutaneous port was placed to facilitate chemo administration; the first of my six-infusion started August 24, 2023, and ran over 8 hours.

PRAYING PASTORS:

A few days before starting chemotherapy, I asked my pastors if they'd come and pray for me; they gladly came and prayed over me, thus obeying James 5:13-15.

"Are any of you suffering hardships? You should pray. Are any of you happy? You should sing praises. Are any of you sick? You should call for the elders of the church to come and pray over you, anointing you with oil in the name of the Lord. Such a prayer offered in faith will make you well. And if you have committed any sins, you will be forgiven."

I believe God answered all these prayers, because He is faithful. He never goes back on promises He had made to His children. Isn't it wonderful to have a Father like we do? He is a merciful Father and the source of all comfort. He comforts us in our afflictions, so we can comfort others. When others are troubled, we will be able to give them the same comfort God has given us (see 2 Corinthians 1:3-4). The peace that comes with this is overwhelming. If you are reading this, and you are not yet a child of God, I encourage you to become one today.

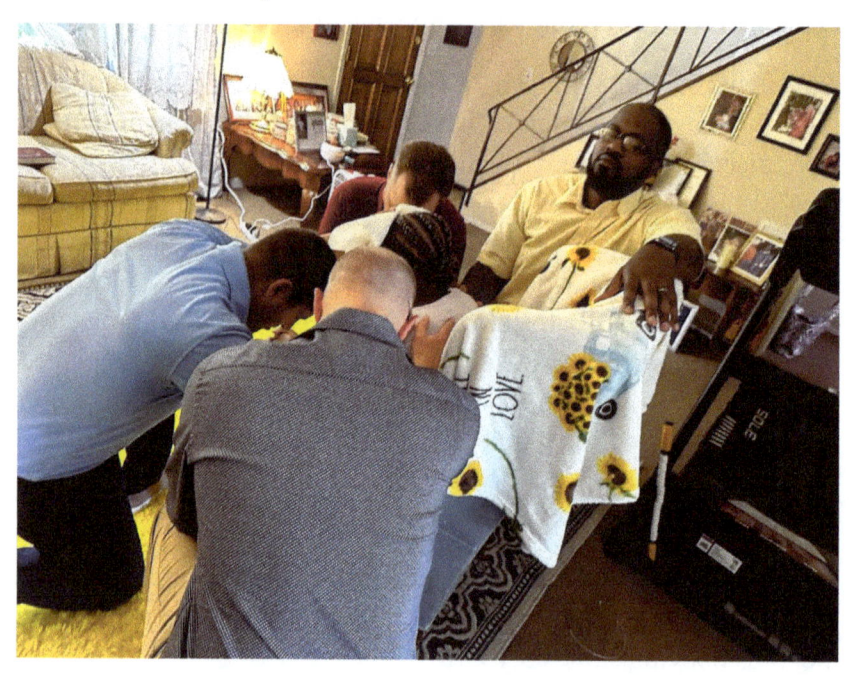

In Remission, Whoot, Whoot!

Later, I obtained an abdominal scan for another reason, and that showed the abdominal lesions were diminished in size! At the midpoint of my treatment regimen (after three doses), my PET SCAN showed no lesions in the abdomen or chest; I was in remission! GOD IS GOOD! Although we were claiming remission, I continued the treatment until I'd gotten all six prescribed doses.

My Chemo Side Effects

But chemotherapy, as a dear friend appropriately called it, is 'A Poison of Healing.' In addition to killing cancer cells, it kills some of the healthy cells in other parts of the body as well, causing all kinds of side effects in a recipient's body. Fortunately, everyone does not experience every known side effect. Personally, I experienced fatigue, brain fog, loss of appetite, numbness of fingertips and lips, difficulty in getting my words out, lack of concentration with reading, discoloration of palms, soles and tongue, weight and hair loss. Below is the evidence of my hair loss:

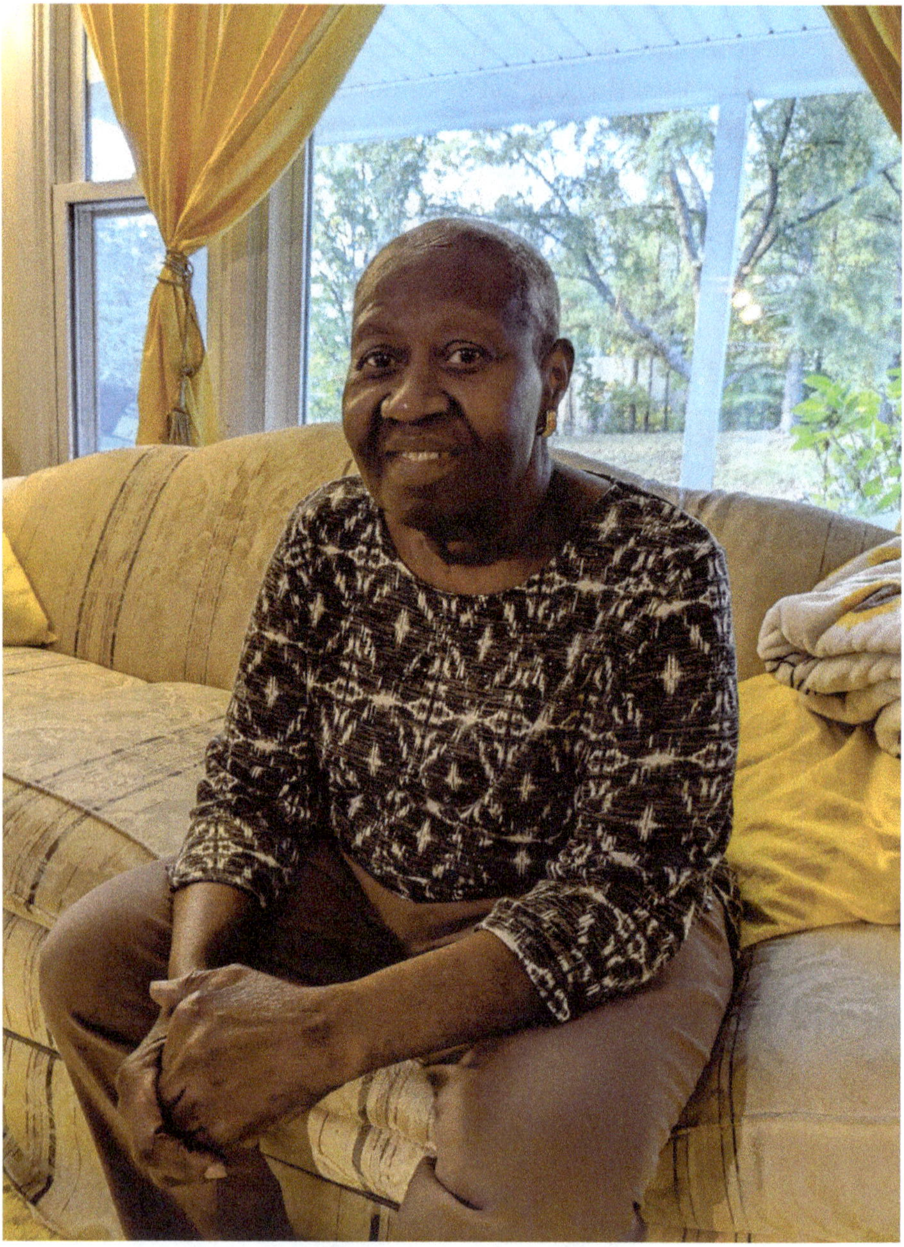

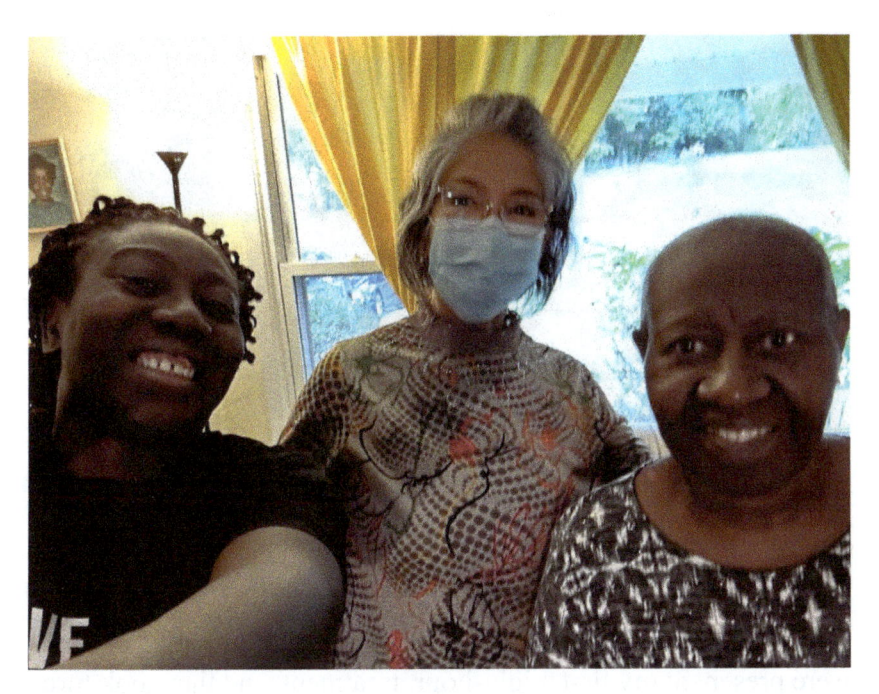

With all that said, let's look at God's promises in all of this.

THE ABUNDANT LIFE

God promised in John 10:10, "The thief's purpose is to steal and kill and destroy. My purpose is to give them a rich and satisfying life." (NLT). Eternal life is not only living forever with Him in heaven someday; it is also for us to live a satisfying life here through our trials while we wait for our heavenly home.

Our satisfying life here on earth includes all that we'll need here: family, friends, health, sustenance, protection, provision, etc. God provided me with all of these plus a lot more.

Below are pictures of my kind and loving family before treatment, mid-treatment, and at the end of treatment.

They spruced up my space to brighten it up: all three of my kids were present at my first, eight-hour, treatment, and they took turns sitting with me. They made sure at least one of them was present during doctor visits, either in person or via a telehealth visit. They took notes and asked questions. They made sure someone was with me 24/7; they wouldn't let me lift a finger. They asked me questions like: what do you need, what are you doing or where are going? They were and are still a big source of encouragement to me and to each other.

What A Difference A Year Makes; It's My Birthday Again - 2023

My 2023 birthday celebration was quite different from the year before: In 2022, I had a head full of hair, and had lunch with family and friends at a restaurant; in 2023, family and friends celebrated me at my home, although I had a poor appetite. With a poor appetite, I couldn't eat much of anything anyway. But thank God, though I was bald-headed, I was alive and celebrated by my church and work families.

Friends sent cards and gifts to encourage me, stopped by to visit, and brought food. I'd never had so much food in the house (not that I could eat much of it anyway). A couple of times, I even had to give some of the food away.

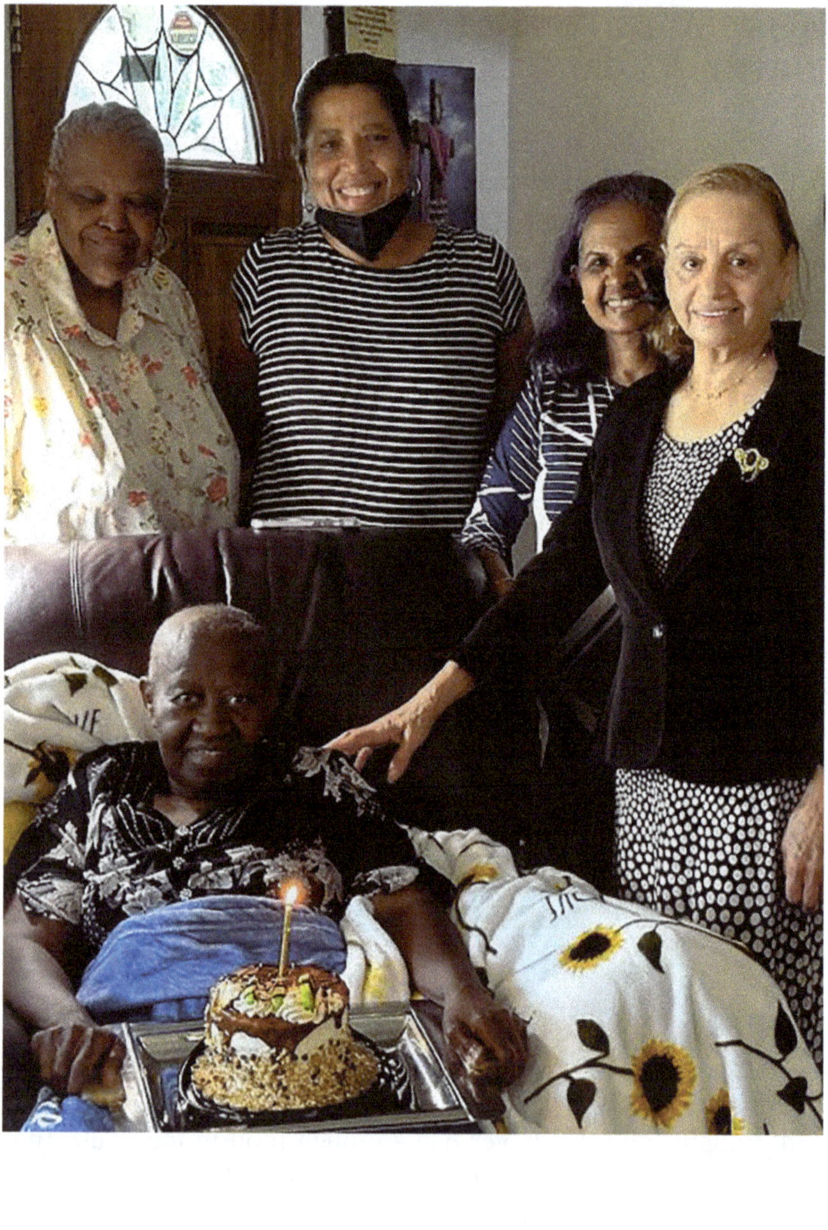

Mid treatment was around Thanksgiving:

GOD'S PROVISION

When I say friends, I mean friends! They prayed from all around the world: the USA, Ghana, Canada, Pakistan, Japan, Romania, etc. These praying friends, including my church family, have been blessed just as much as I have been; they experienced God answering their prayers in wonderful ways on my behalf, and rather quickly. I saw my pain work together for my good and the good of all those who were praying; through this, we have all learned to trust God more. After all, if we didn't have problems, how would we know He could solve them, and how would He get the glory?

Last Day Of Treatment – December 7, 2023

At the completion of my last infusion, I walked out into the hallway thinking I was going to ring the bell and be on my way home. To my surprise, the hallway was full; my family, church family, pastors, and friends had come to celebrate my discharge and watch me ring the bell. The hospital staff, so surprised by how many visitors came, said to my family: "That must be a very important patient." Yes, I was, and I'm still important to God, family, and friends!

Here are my pastors and friends who came to celebrate my discharge and watch me ring the bell; their coming was a surprise arranged by my family.

I am sure my care team at the hospital was hand-picked by God; they were so loving and caring. They were kind, respectful, patient, and encouraging. See pictures below:

My oncologist was tied up on my last treatment day when I was scheduled to ring the bell: still, he somehow managed to look around to find me and wish me well. He named us Team Pearl because my children were always with me; I never visited alone.

The staff treated me like family! They called me by name, smiled, asked how I was doing, etc.—they showed and expressed genuine interest in my well-being. What a blessing.

IS IT OR IS IT NOT OVER?

I'm Home Now

The family brought me home on December seventh with a list of all kinds of follow-up appointments. At home, I was so pampered! My children continued to make sure I lacked nothing they could provide; they got a clothes heater to ensure my towels, clothes, and socks were warm, since I felt cold most of the time. They kissed me countless times per day. Even their friends, both known and unknown to me, sent cards and gifts. What a mighty Provider God is; He provides through people.

At the end of chemotherapy, I assumed I was all done. PRAISE THE LORD! But oh, not so fast! Some of the side effects lingered on: memory fog especially; my computer skills disappeared, I couldn't remember names, and in addition, exhaustion became my middle name; I was always tired, short of breath, and feeling the need to sit or lay down. Follow-up x-rays and scans showed an enlarged heart (cardiomegaly), and fluid in the chest. The radiologist's impression was congestive heart failure with pulmonary edema that had slightly progressed since prior scans (3/2/24). I was prescribed diuretics to drain the fluid in the chest. That wasn't fun, but God sustained me through all of it. I'm grateful to God for all He's brought me through.

Dear Reader, here's a question for you. What do you think about my God? Is He your God as well? And if He's not, how would you cope with this kind of situation if it ever happened to you or a loved one? I think it will be better for you to be in a relationship with Him now, where you already know and trust Him. Below is the process by which you can know Him:

It all starts with the understanding that we are all sinners (see Romans 3:23) and that the payment, or result, of sin is eternal separation from God in hell. On the other hand, a personal relationship with God leads to eternal life with God in heaven (see Romans 6:23). God sent His son, Jesus, to take our punishment on Himself, which is why Christ died. So, if we repent of our sins, ask for God's forgiveness, and put our faith in Jesus, who died in our place, God forgives us and makes us His children, starting a personal relationship between us and Him. If you'd want to become His child, pray the prayer below sincerely:

> *"Dear God, I know I'm a sinner, and I ask for your forgiveness. I believe Jesus Christ is Your Son. I believe that He died for my sin and that you raised Him to life. I want to trust Him as my Savior and follow Him as Lord from this day forward. Guide my life and help me to do your will. I pray this in the name of Jesus. Amen."*

If you pray this prayer sincerely, God will hear and answer you. He will put His Spirit in your heart as confirmation that you've become His child, and a guarantee that you'll inherit heaven. Having begun that Father/child relationship, you have the assurance that He will meet all your needs according to His will and plans for your life, and eventually bring you home to heaven to live forever with Him.

You'll have to grow in your relationship through daily Bible reading, prayer, and obedience to what the Bible says. Joining a local body of Bible believers for fellowship will also grow your faith.

Being in an ongoing relationship with God will help you to trust and depend on Him all the time, whether or not you have problems. So, what do you think, Dear Reader? Are you ready to submit to His leadership? Even if you never get sick like I did, you still have to be concerned about where you'll go to spend eternity when you die. Decide now, while you have time, because time is running out.

CHRISTMAS 2023 WITH FAMILY

I celebrated Christmas with my beloved family. See us below; I was alive and had a smile. The family was overjoyed. God has been faithful, just like we knew He would be.

More pictures for your enjoyment!

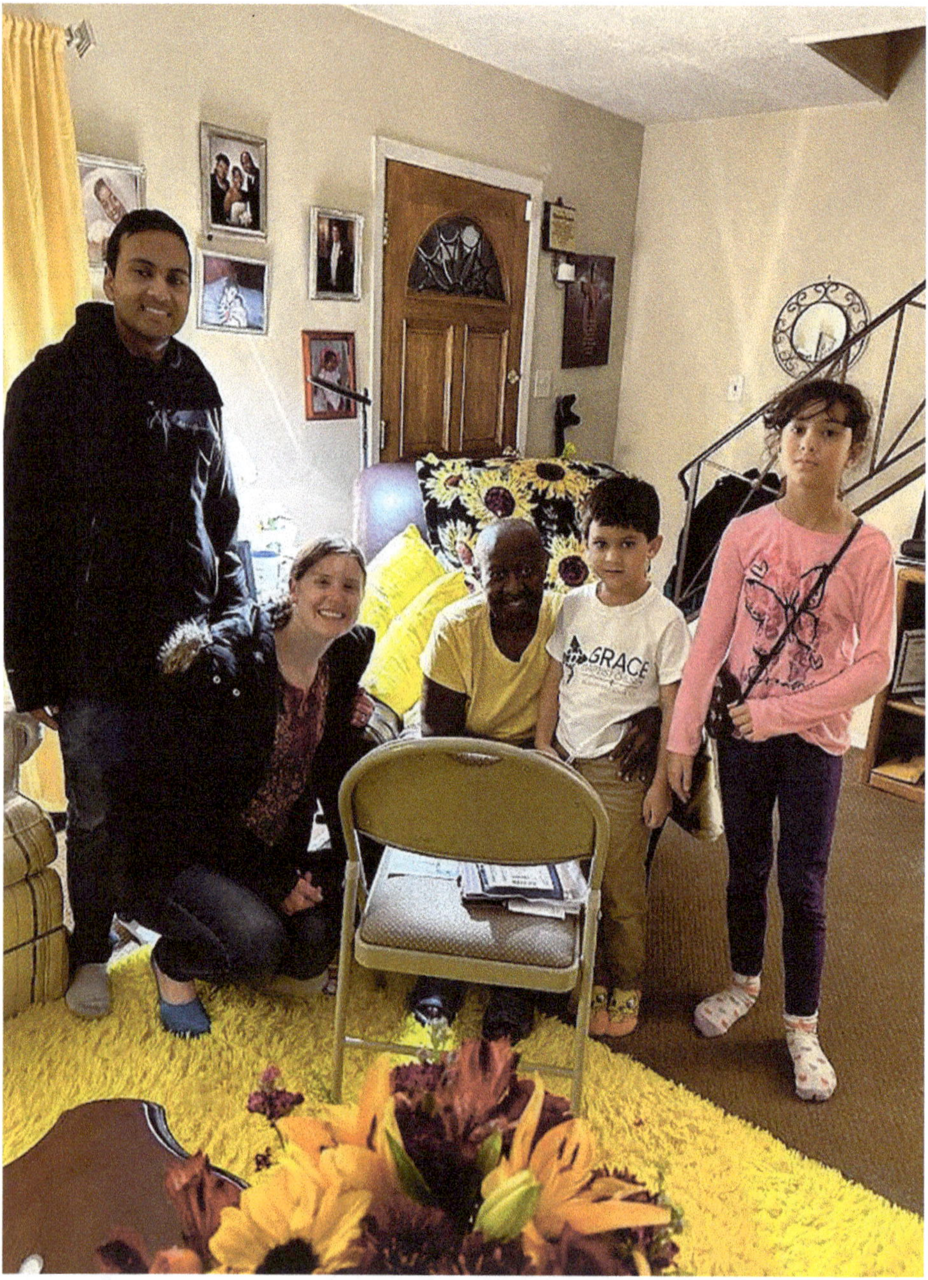
GRACE

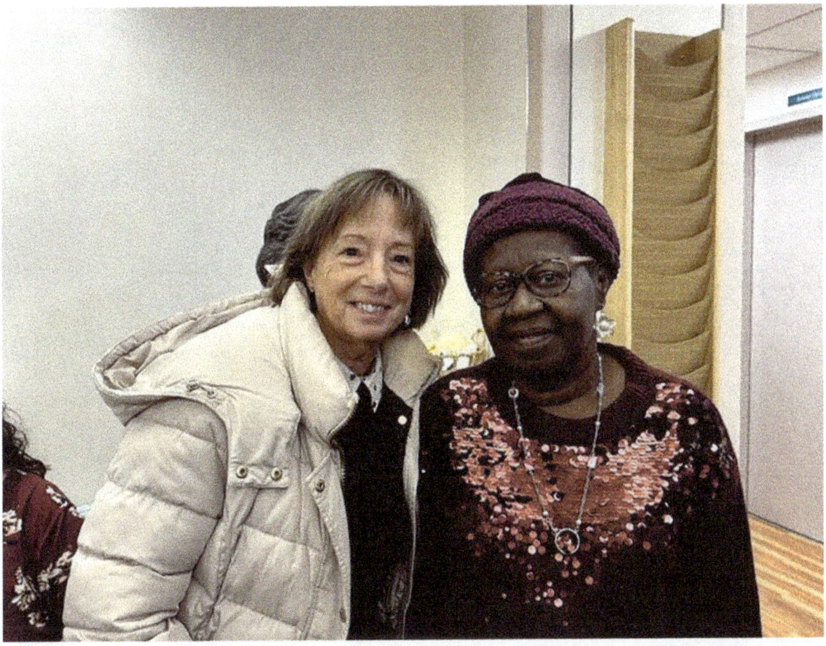

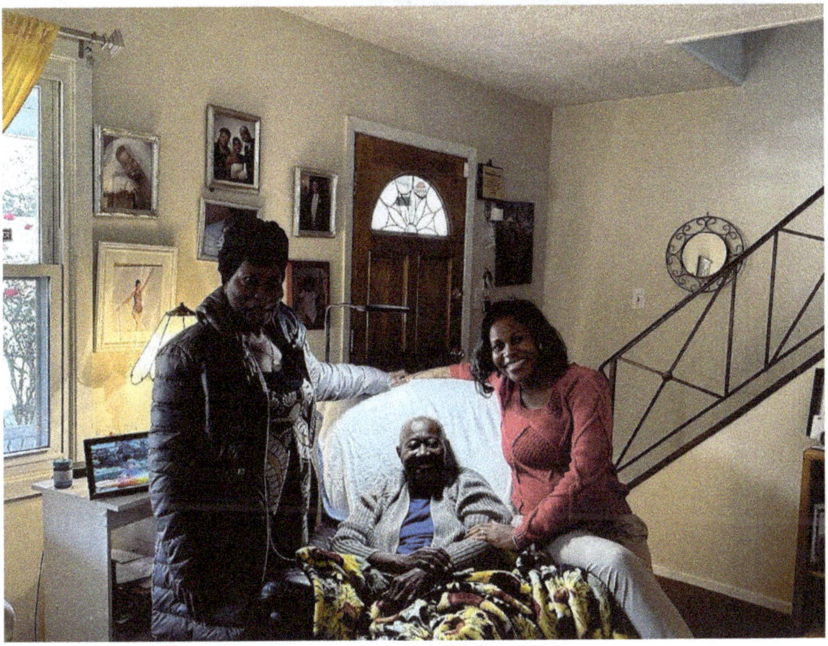

24

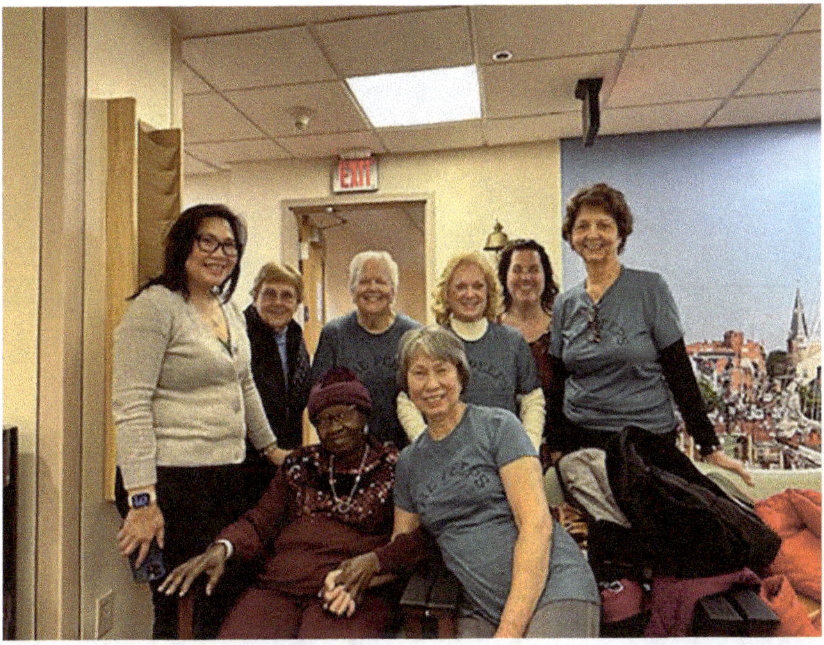
EXIT

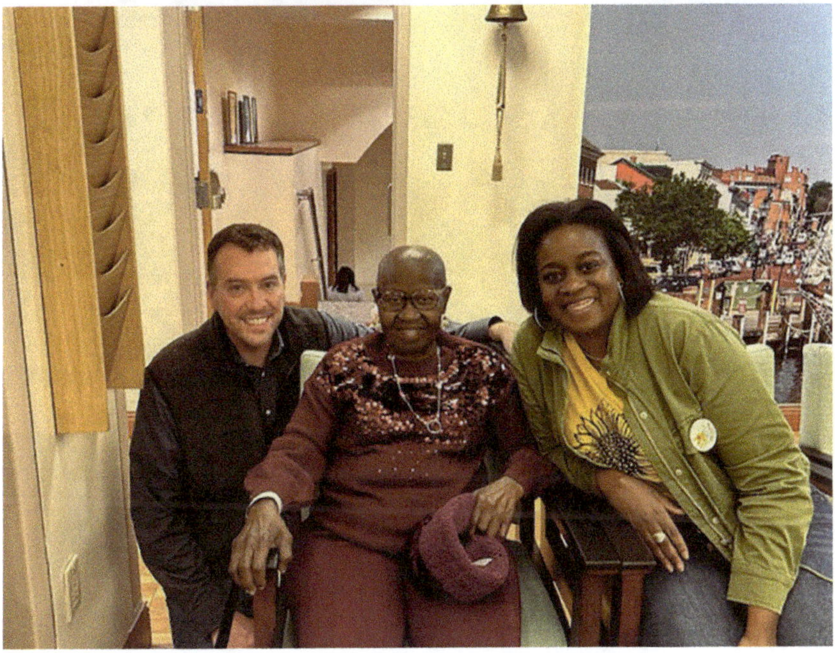

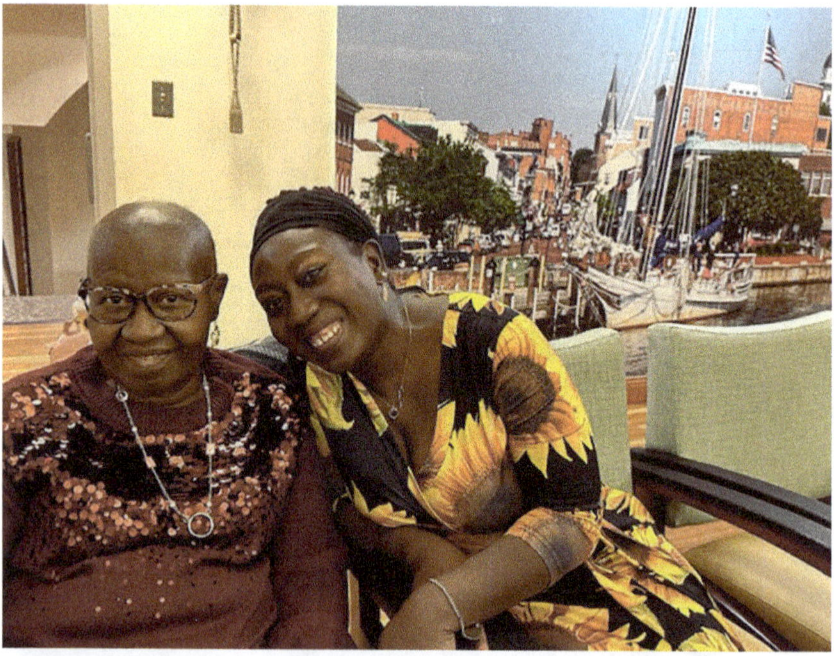

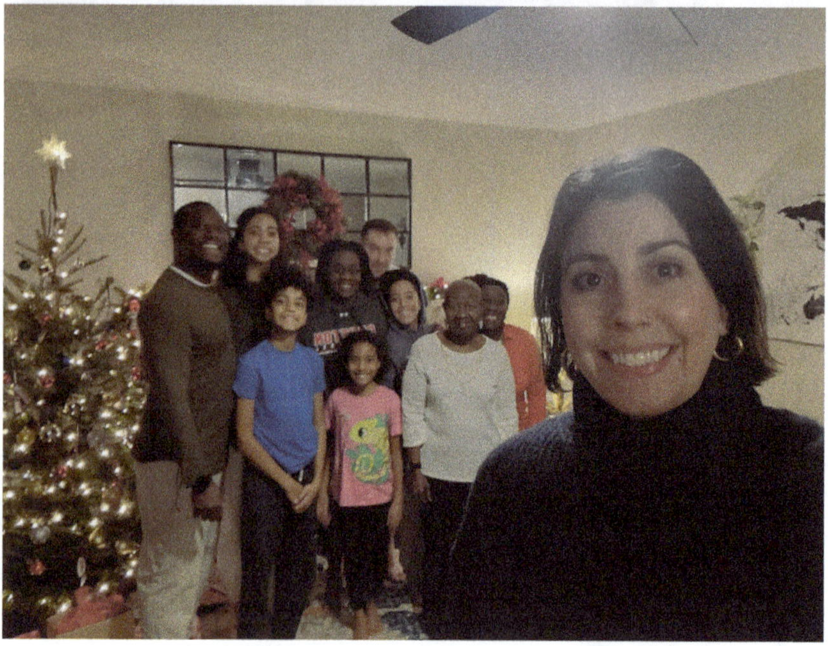

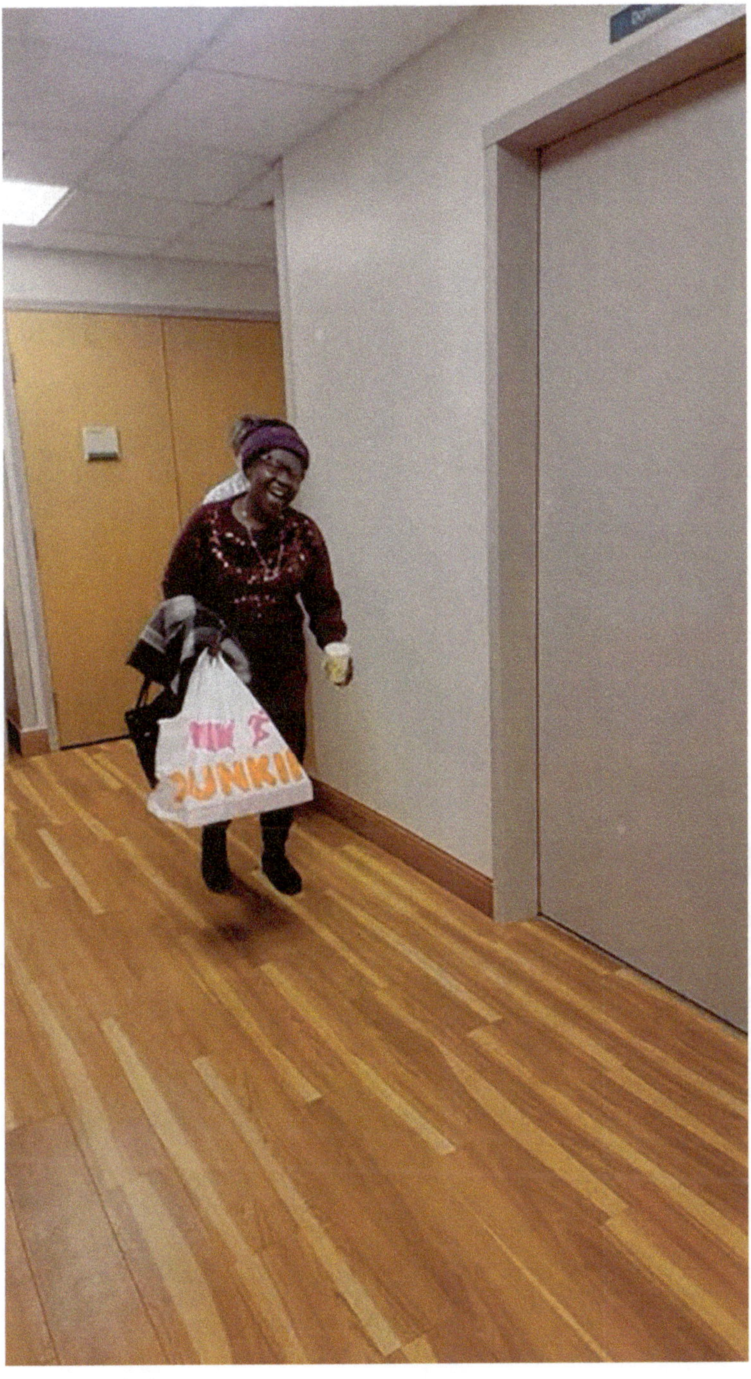

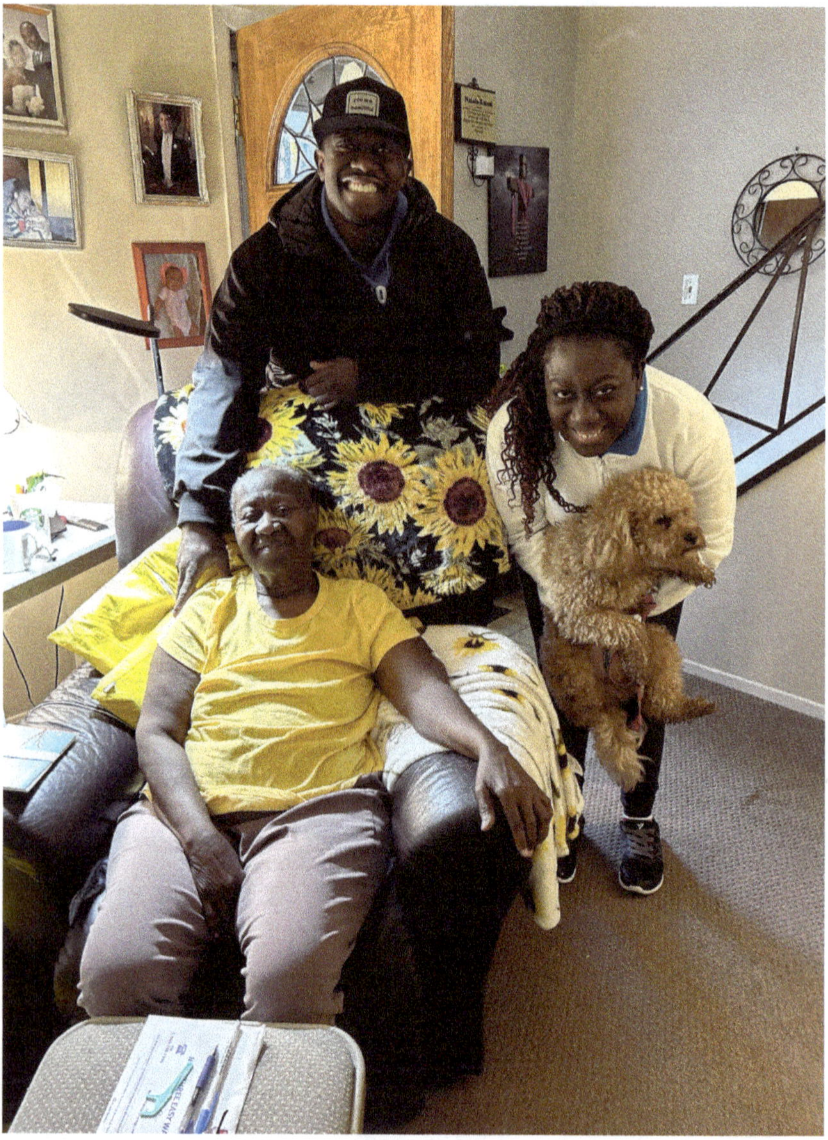

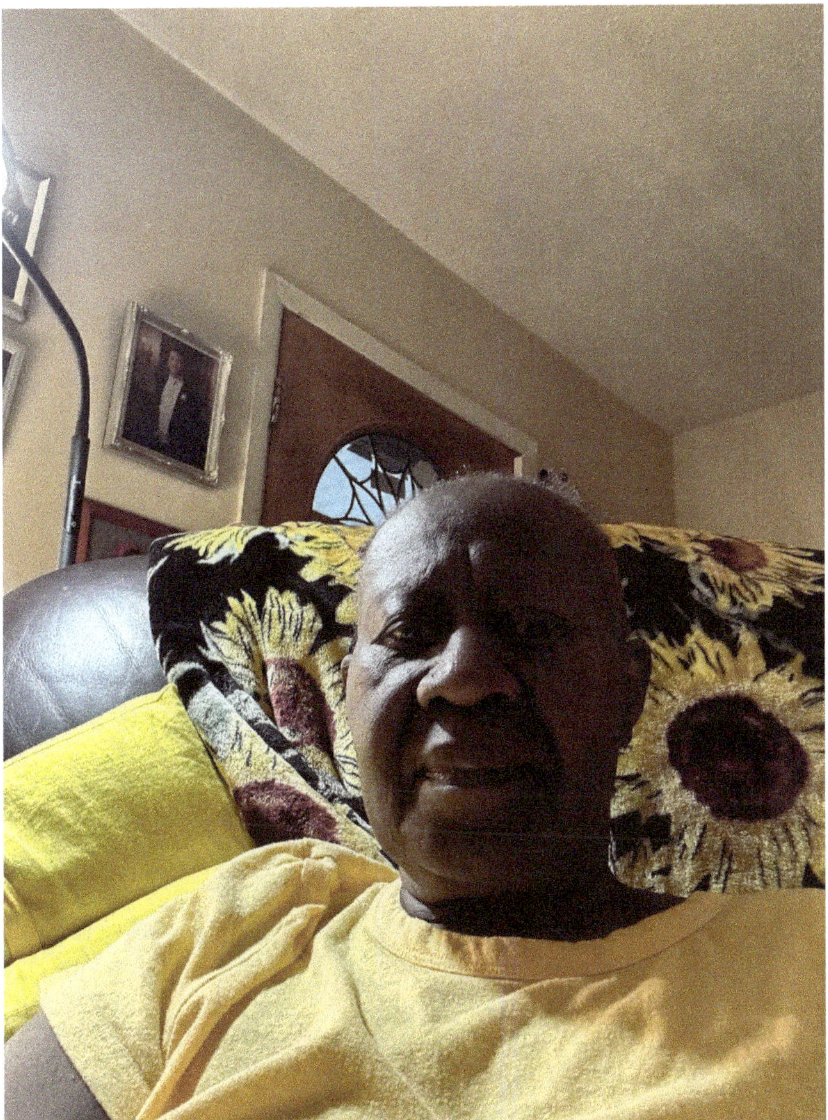

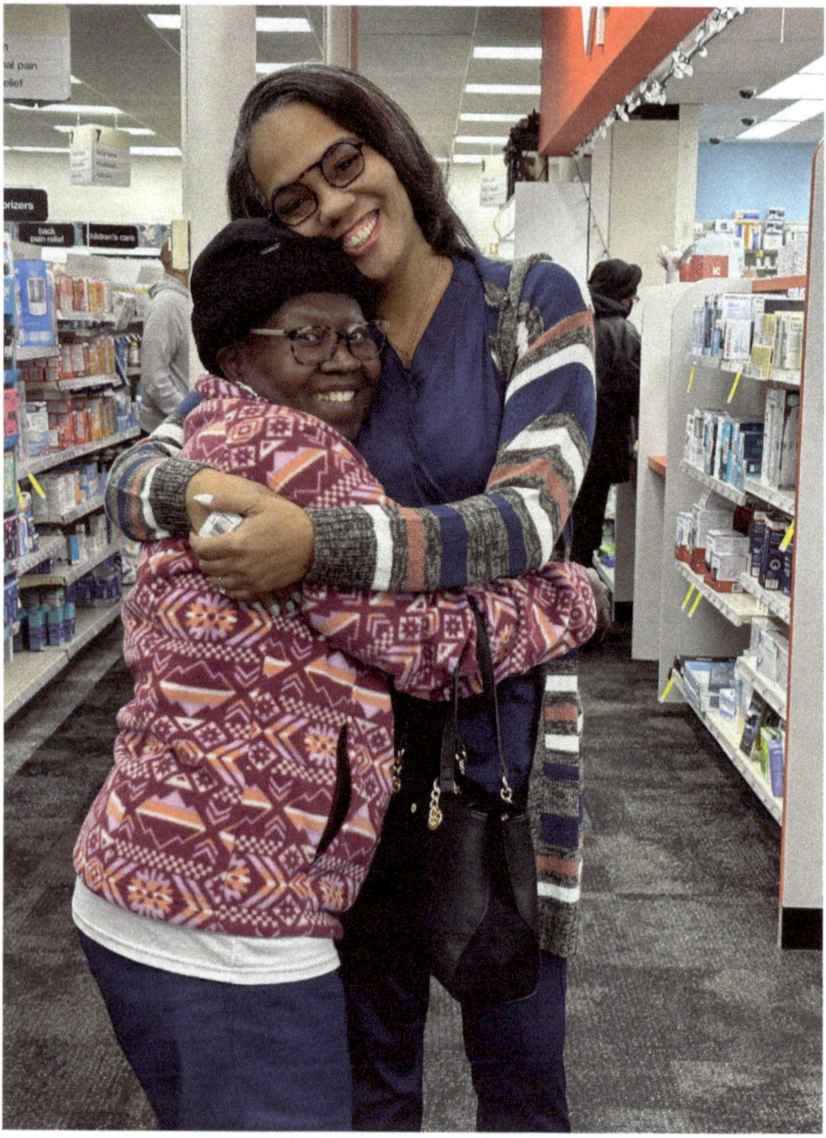

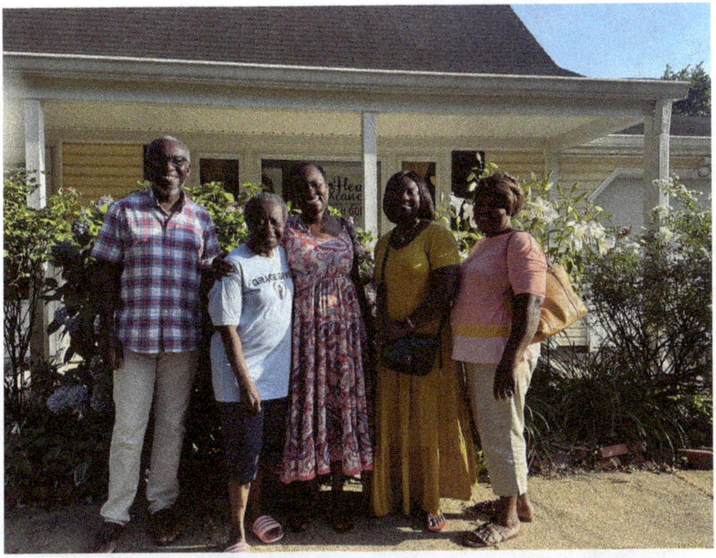

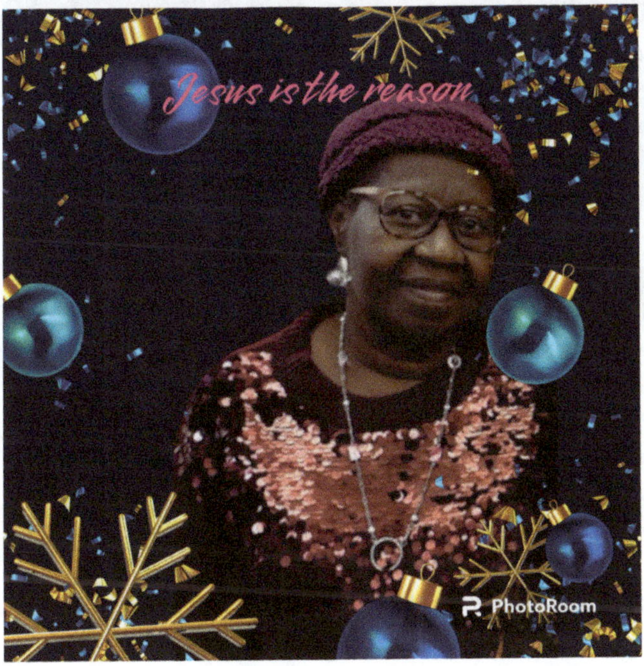
Jesus is the reason
PhotoRoom

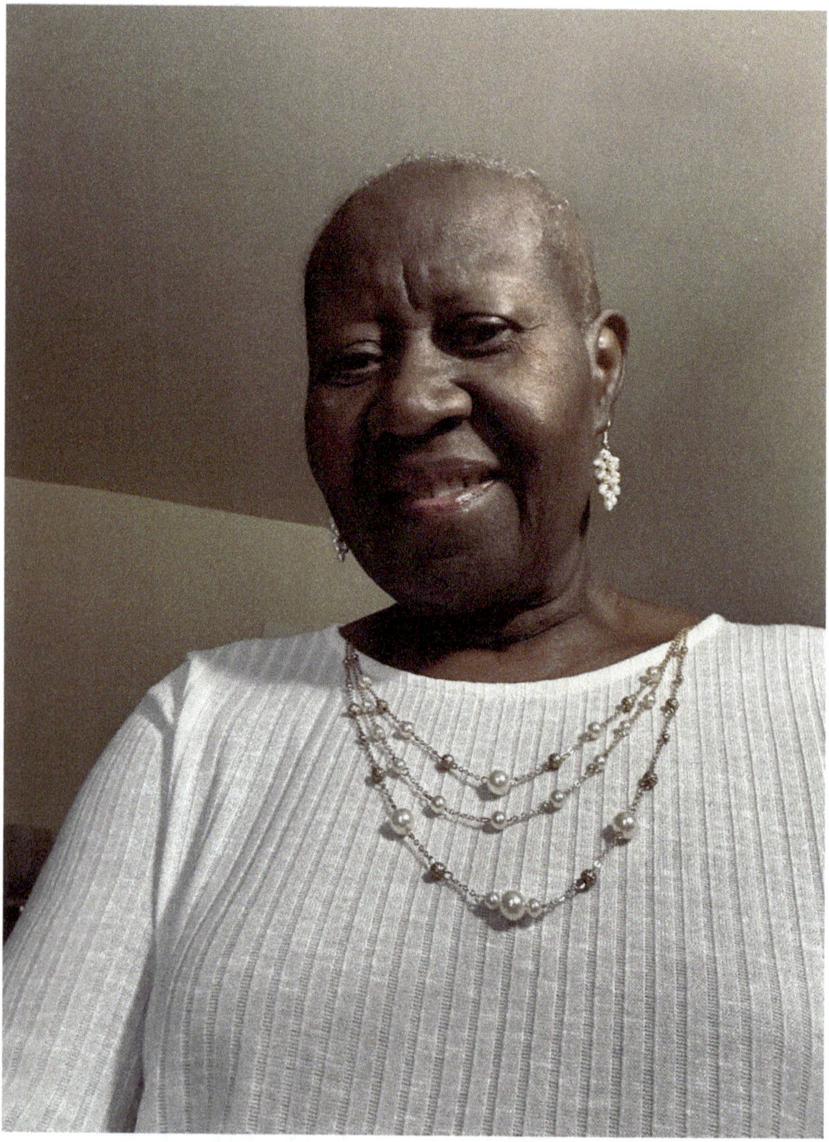

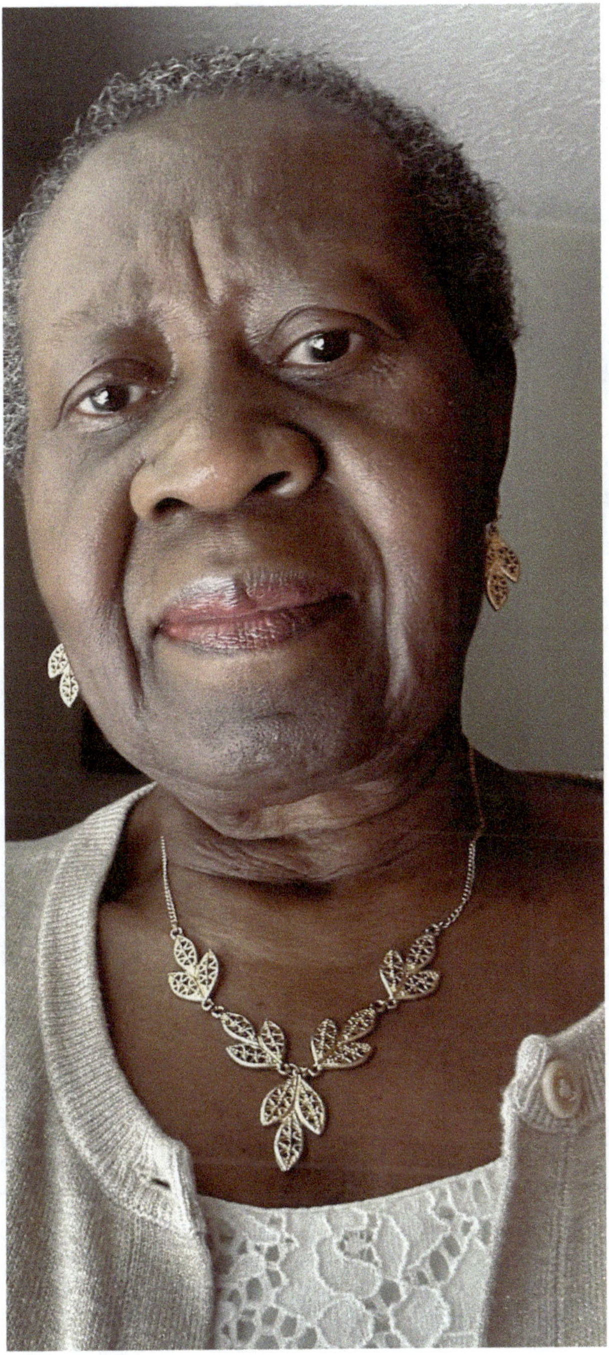

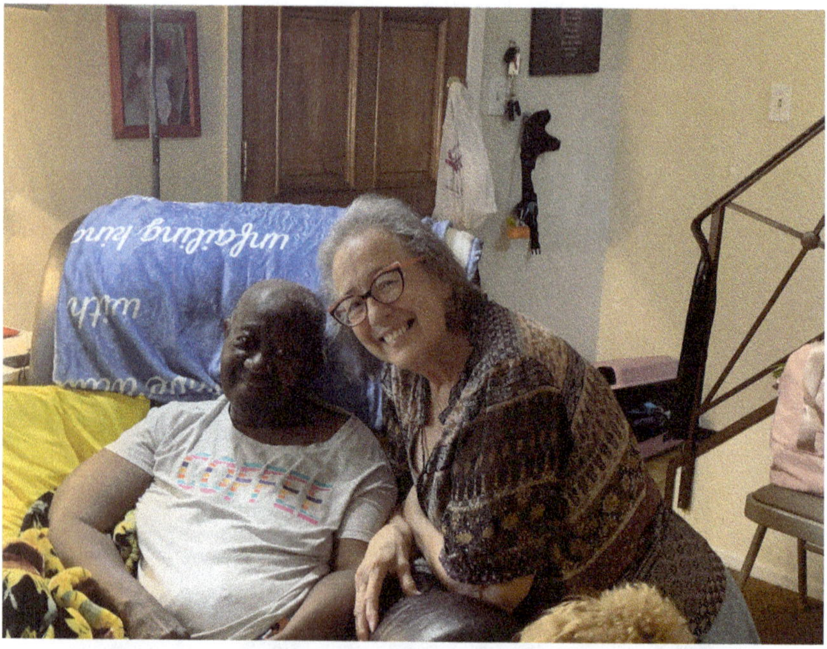
COFFEE

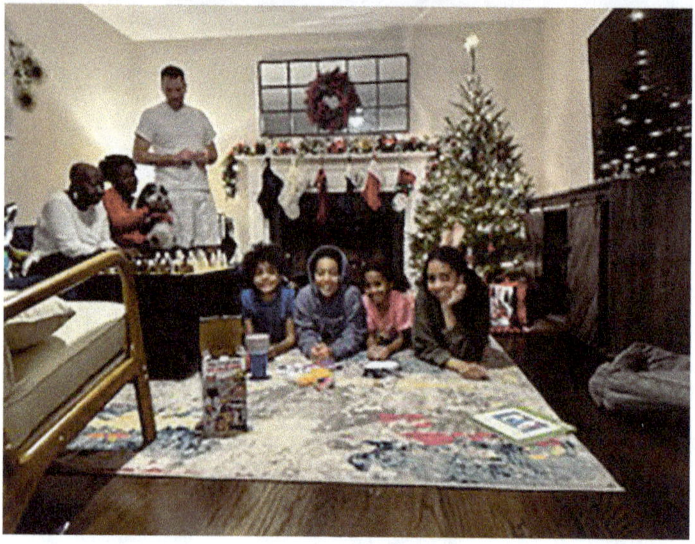

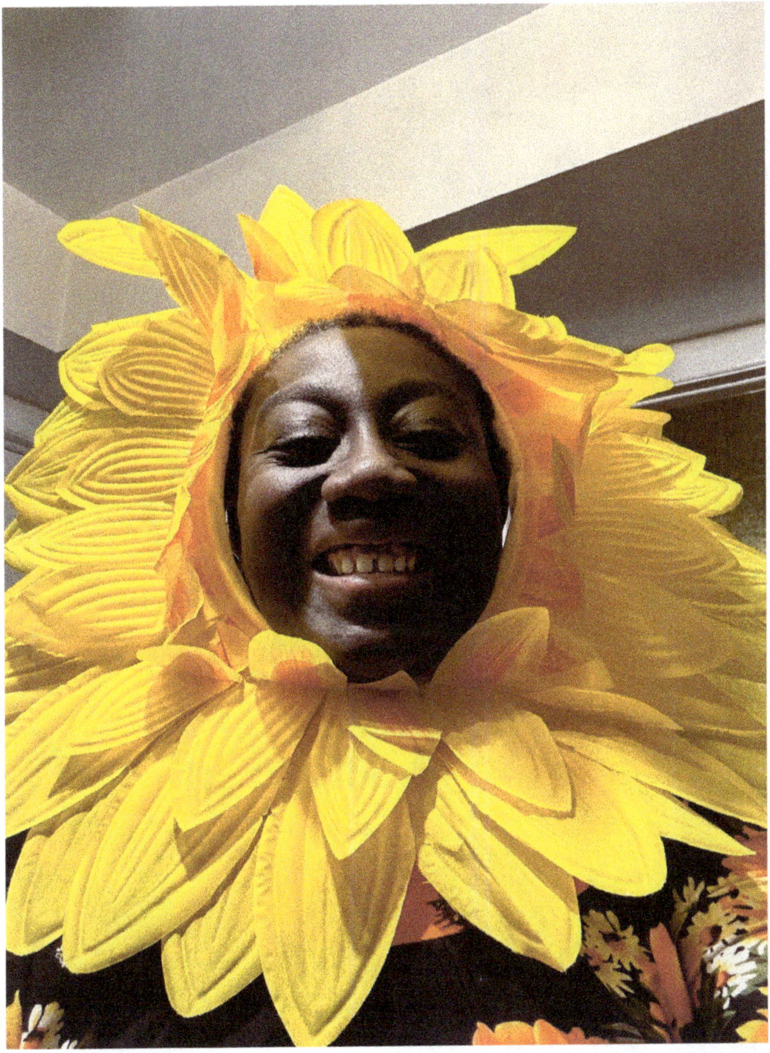

36

Six Months After Treatment

So, it's been six months since I completed chemotherapy but most of the side effects are still ongoing. The worst being memory fog and weight loss. As I write this, I don't feel as exhausted and my hair is growing, and my appetite has improved. God continues to provide me with His overwhelming peace for which I am very grateful. How long is it going to take until I'm completely whole? I have no idea; I hear it could take up to a year. All I know is, "Let God be true though every one were a liar" (Romans 3:4). I still have specialists' appointments to keep, scans and x-rays to undergo, and medications to take. Either way, I'll continue to trust God and rest in His overwhelming peace!

Printed in the USA
CPSIA information can be obtained
at www.ICGtesting.com
CBHW070230091224
18682CB00007B/64